Floors and Flooring

Homes & Ideas

Floors and Flooring

Annie Ashworth

BXTREE

Welcome to the *Homes & Ideas* book of *Floors and Flooring*. *Homes & Ideas* is the magazine for bright, creative and budget-conscious home style and is packed with informative and inspiring ideas. Lifestyles and homes are constantly changing, and with them are the needs of our readers. More ideas, more information and more easy-to-follow projects are always in demand, and it was this demand which has prompted the idea of a series of books covering in greater detail the most popular topics featured in *Homes & Ideas*. *Floors and Flooring* is the definitive guide to choosing the correct flooring throughout the home – let's face it, the choice today is absolutely huge and we all need help to avoid making what can be a costly mistake! All topics to do with flooring are covered, from restoring and painting wooden floors and what to expect from different types of carpeting, to an in-depth look at more unusual floor coverings and achieving stunning effects with mosaics and brickwork. No room has been forgotten and there are hundreds of ideas for living areas, bathrooms, kitchens and bedrooms. It is a perfect partner for *Homes & Ideas* and will provide you with all the answers to the most popular questions regarding the best flooring for your home – wherever you live.

Debbie Djordjevic
Editor – *Homes & Ideas*

Contents

Introduction

For most people, choosing flooring can be the hardest decorating decision of them all: it has to serve so many purposes in so many places in the home; it can be shrouded in technicalities; usually demands the services of a professional to lay; and, worst of all, it can be very costly.

This book will take the fear out of flooring. It is full of ideas and information to help you decide which types of flooring will suit the different parts of your home – and suit your budget as well. Once you have a good idea of what you are looking for, *Floors and Flooring* will guide you through all the choices available – natural stone, wood or matting, the latest in vinyl and the very wide (and sometimes rather bewildering) selection of carpeting.

Easy step-by-step instructions will show you how to lay the floors you can tackle yourself, and we'll tell you when it's better to call in the experts. Finally, as most of us have to inherit (and live with) the flooring chosen by the people who lived in our house before us, *Floors and Flooring* shows you how to restore neglected flooring to its former glory, and how to keep your new flooring looking as good as new.

1 Choosing the right floor

The floor takes up a huge area of a room, and has to fulfil different functions in different rooms. In a kitchen it should be practical and easy to clean; in a sitting room or playroom it should be comfortable to sit on and play on; in the bedroom it should have a warm, welcoming feel when you step out of bed each morning.

As well as having to put up with a large amount of traffic trekking over it day in and day out, the floor forms the basis for the rest of the room decoration. It can bring colours together, act as a backdrop, or, if it is interesting enough, be the centre of attention itself. What is more, your flooring will probably out-live several changes in the surrounding decoration.

Flooring need not be restricted to a single type or colour in one room. Large rugs can be laid over a beautifully painted or polished wooden floor. Natural matting can be covered in colourful kilims. Vinyl can have a decorative and contrasting border. A ceramic tiled kitchen floor might lead out to a terracotta tiled conservatory beyond. The choices are possibly much wider than you realised. They are, in fact, as wide as your imagination.

Of course, some floor coverings will be ruled out immediately as unsuitable – the best Wilton carpet is not a very practical choice for the kitchen, neither is a tiled floor for the bedroom, unless you live in a hot dry climate. However, every year manufacturers are improving the quality of their products, making them more hard wearing, more versatile and avail-able in an ever larger choice of colours.

Perhaps of all the furnishings and fixtures we choose, a floor will show its quality quickest, although this does not necessarily mean the most expensive floor is the best. Yet if there is one golden rule in choosing flooring, it is that you should select the best you can afford. Short cuts will show, and are a false economy. In no time at all you will have to repair or replace the flooring, when, if you had stretched yourself a little more when you first laid it, you would still have a beautiful floor in good condi-tion to show for your trouble.

9

CHECKLIST

This is designed to help you choose the type of flooring you prefer, and the one that would be the most practical. It will help you whittle down the vast list of choices, making your final decision an easier one.
- **What type of activities will take place in the room – cooking, washing, sleeping, playing with toys, bathing, sitting on the floor?**
- **Is it an area that will be subject to heavy use, such as a hallway, the area in front of a sideboard, bath or lavatory?**
- **Is it near an outside door?**
- **Will the flooring be splashed with water; are pets likely to walk and lie on it; will prams or bikes be pushed over it?**
- **Does the flooring have to work with the period of the house or an existing style or colour scheme?**
- **Should the flooring provide heat or noise insulation?**
- **Is the floor strong enough to take the weight of the flooring you have chosen?**
- **Do you need to prepare or repair the floor before you lay the new flooring?**

The right floor for the right room

Once you have gone through the checklist you will realise it is possible to have a different floor covering for each room in the house, such are the different demands of each one. There really are no hard and fast rules, but generally speaking the following choices are the most suitable.

Hallways receive the most traffic in the house; they have to cope with wet, dirty shoes and umbrellas, muddy boots and animals. While flooring must be welcoming, it must also be practical, hard wearing and easy to clean. Wood is a good choice, and good quality hardwood not only lasts for years but also improves with age. Natural stone flooring, perhaps softened with keystones between each tile, is entirely practical and contrasts well with other types of flooring that can be seen in the distance. Vinyl and linoleum is even easier to keep clean and, with the addition of stylish borders, can look smart as well as being practical. The disadvantages of these, and of terracotta tiles (which do need maintenance) is that they can need constant mopping, especially during the winter months. A stain resistant carpet of the hardest-wearing variety will be warm and welcoming, as well as easy to vacuum clean once any mud has dried.

Staircases take the greatest battering, and an unsuitable carpet will show its lack of quality very quickly by wearing on the edges. Left bare, however, stairs can be noisy and slippery. Carpet is an ideal choice, but make sure you have chosen the right weave and quality of carpet, snugly fitted, so it will serve you for years and remain attractive (*see* Chapter 5). Uncarpeted staircases should not be overlooked, however. The wooden stairs found in many 19th-century English cottages were usually left polished or painted. Polishing can be treacherous, but a matt-painted surface can be very effective. Your paint supplier should be able to suggest which is the most suitable matt varnish to protect your work from the wear of feet. Terracotta tiling on each tread is very effective too, with the nose of the tread edged with wood and the risers painted in a plain colour – preferably white. This style can be very attractive, giving the feeling of a traditional villa or simple French cottage.

11

Conservatories and sun rooms are similar to hallways in that they may be the first place muddy feet will land from outside. However, they are also a halfway area – neither house nor garden. Once again most hard flooring will suit because it is easy to keep clean, and because the natural colours of terracotta, slate, or ceramic tiles work well with the plants and flowers that live in a conservatory. These floors will also blend with the natural colours of the garden beyond. Be bold with contrasting keystones or floor patterns that look effective but do not fight with the neutral colours of wicker and wood, which are usually predominant in conservatory furniture.

Living rooms suit wall-to-wall carpeting, the cosiest and most traditional choice, and there is a wide choice of colours which can contribute to your design scheme. For a more contemporary look, natural flooring can be very effective (see Chapter 3 for ideas on coir and sisal matting), particularly when the neutral tones are broken up with rugs in interesting designs and colours. Wooden floors, either in pale pine or beech, or warmer oak and mahogany, look welcoming, and as long as there are no draughty gaps, will be warm enough underfoot.

Kitchen floors need to be hygienic, easy to clean, slip resistant and durable enough to cope with all manner of spillage. The hardest-wearing surfaces are natural stone, ceramic tiles or even wood that has been well sealed. These are easy to brush and wash, but they can be cold and hard underfoot in a room where you may well be doing a lot of standing. Vinyl flooring is a softer choice, and comes in designs that so closely resemble natural materials that it can be hard to tell one from the other. Vinyl is strong (although it can burn), and if you have children, a speckled pattern will cover up the odd crumb that escapes the broom. Carpeting is less practical, although carpet tiles are an option. They can be moved around, so that any stains can be hidden (see Chapter 5). Natural flooring is unsuitable near a source of heat such as an oven or cooker.

Opposite: **Vinyl fulfils the necessary criteria for kitchen flooring: ease of care and resilience. Added to that, it is available in finishes such as teak, shown here, that are hard to tell apart from the real thing.**
Below: **The soft tones of slate, with subtle varieties of colour, provide practical flooring for this kitchen and blend well with the extensive brickwork.**

Bathrooms demand a waterproof floor cover with a non-slip finish. A carpet is a soft option for the room in which you are most likely to pad about in bare feet, but it must be rubber backed, and really needs the ventilation a larger bathroom can provide. Another disadvantage of carpeting is that it can become very unhygienic around the lavatory. As most British bathrooms are very small (2.4 x 1.8m on average), cork, vinyl, rubber and linoleum are more suitable solutions. All four are soft and warm, can withstand being wet and are easy to disinfect. The bathroom is a good place to have fun with pattern and design, and a small surface area that needs covering may allow you to be a bit more extravagant with the flooring you choose. Because of the damp conditions and heavy use, bathroom flooring is probably replaced more often than anywhere else, so there is even more reason to make a good investment initially.

Vinyl flooring in a bathroom offers a practical surface which is easy to wipe and comes in a wide selection of finishes, such as this sophisticated marbled design, at a fraction of the cost of the real thing.

17

Wooden flooring, while somewhat unconventional in a bedroom, is ideal for people who suffer from dust allergies, as it can be wiped clean.

Bedrooms take the least traffic (unless perhaps it doubles up as a child's playroom) so the flooring can be less expensive than elsewhere, and carpeting is the most welcoming under the feet on a cold winter's morning. Don't economise too much however, because some areas, such as around the bed, dressing table or mirror, will take quite a bit of wear and tear. Wood, cork or cushioned vinyl flooring covered with rugs is another possibility and, because all three are easy to wet-wipe clean, are ideal for those who are sensitive to dust or have asthma.

Children's rooms benefit from carpeting; it is the warm, comforting choice for the same reasons as it is in an adult's bedroom. However, if your children will be playing much of the time in their room, and even if the carpeting is stain resistant, you might need to plump for a flooring that is more practical and hard wearing. Cork, which has been correctly sealed, and vinyl will cope with spills (even paint and glue), and are warm enough surfaces for children to sit on and play. Wooden floors work too, especially if they are painted in fun colours to co-ordinate with the room, but can be noisy under the feet of boisterous children.

Buying flooring

The checklist on page 9 will have helped you to reduce your choice, so now the array of flooring available will seem less daunting. Stick to your plans – even if you just know what you don't want, and not yet what you do – and you are less likely to be overwhelmed. When you are ready to buy the flooring, keep the following points in mind:

• The advantage of the larger carpet and flooring retailers is that they offer a wide choice, but make sure that quality has not been sacrificed in order to offer you tantalisingly cheap deals. The smaller the retailer the more likely they are to be able to give you professional advice.

• You will need to take along a large swatch of any furnishing fabric you want to co-ordinate with your flooring.

• Always ask for the largest possible sample of a carpet, or for several tiles, so you can take them home to try in the room.

• Make sure you know exactly what is included in the price on offer (laying, underlay for carpets, etc.) and don't necessarily settle for the fittings and types of underlay that the retailer is offering.

• Decide on the style of skirting you would like to use if there isn't any in the room.

• Think about what you will put in the junctions between rooms and on the nose of stair treads.

• Make a note of any special cleaning instructions for your chosen flooring.

• Make sure your calculations are as correct as possible. Most tile companies, for example, will not accept returns if you miscalculate.

• Check that colour and pattern are consistent in a tile batch or carpet before it is laid.

• Always check whether the professional who is laying your floor is able to remove and take away the old flooring. Otherwise you will have to make your own arrangements.

Tricks with flooring

Flooring can play an important part in your design scheme. A single colour will help to unify the other patterns and colours in the room, and can fulfil other functions as well. Medium and pale shades will make small floor areas look more spacious, while dark colours will be warmer and cosier – and show less dirt. (See Chapter 5 on how to choose the right colour for carpeting.) Colour will unify two rooms as well. If a conservatory or sun room leads off a kitchen, flooring of a similar tone, even if made from different material, will help to make the rooms seems less disjointed. A small house or flat will look less busy, and therefore larger, if as much of the same carpet or flooring as possible is used throughout. This is made easier now that some manufacturers produce carpeting in the same shade but in differing weights for different situations.

Design can also alter the apparent dimensions of a room. Tiles laid in broad lines or laid diagonally can make a narrow kitchen look broader, and a border, either painted on wood, within a carpet pattern or created with the clever use of tiles, can help to draw in the walls of a wide room. Similarly, patterned carpeting will help to reduce the dimensions of a room (see Chapter 5 for more ideas).

19

2 Hard floors

Hard flooring is exactly that – solid and uncushioned – so at worst it is cold and ungiving underfoot. Yet the great advantage of hard flooring, which includes bricks, natural stone, terracotta tiles, slate and marble, is that it will outlast all other types and will actually improve with age. You need only look at the stone hallways and kitchens in houses several centuries old to see how the constant traffic of feet has softened the edges and mellowed the colour.

Brick and terracotta have a warmer colour than cooler marble or creamy limestone, but the latter are very hard wearing and ideal for hallways and kitchens.

Any hard flooring is difficult to lay, needing a completely flat surface, and in most cases it is advisable to call in an expert. More importantly, hard flooring is extremely heavy, which makes it unsuitable for use on anything but a ground floor, unless you have been assured by a building surveyor that the floor can sup-port the weight, and you take pains to support a timber floor if it is not strong enough (see page 40).

Types of hard flooring

Natural stone (main picture below), which includes marble, limestone and slate, has been quarried from the earth as a whole piece, and is then cut, riven or chiselled into shape.

Marble (inset) is very hard wearing and is available with a worn-looking or shiny appearance, the latter harder to lay. Although marble can be cold underfoot, and really quite noisy, it comes in marvellous colours, from white veined in grey, to a myriad of reds, ochres and greens. Prices vary enormously, and it can be an expensive material unless you use it as thin sheets or tiles, which are laid in cement on concrete, or on a strong, level wooden floor. Marble is easy to care for and is a low maintenance material.

22

Granite is as hard wearing as marble, and very durable, although not much less expensive. It comes in a wide range of colours from white through to greens, blues, reds and black. Again, it is low maintenance, and its durability makes it perfect for places where there is a lot of traffic.

Slate (above) can be noisy, hard to handle and usually expensive, but for all that the range of beautiful colours – from blue-greys to pinks and ambers – as well as its compatibility with other types of flooring, may persuade you to put up with its disadvantages.

Brick offers more colour choice than the ubiquitous terracotta browns and reds. You can find yellows, greens, blues and even purples. Brick is warmer underfoot than any of the hard floorings mentioned above, is non-slip, waterproof and stain and grease resistant. It is also an ideal material for continuing from a kitchen or hall to a conservatory, terrace or garden (as long as bricks used outside are frost proof). Bricks are a relatively cheap material, and quite easy to lay yourself, providing they are laid on a damp-proof course and into a flat mortar bed with mortar joining (some can be laid on thin adhesive). Check with your supplier about sealing them.

Stone can either be limestone, York stone or sandstone quarried whole and cut to shape (see **granite**), or stoneware, which refers to a chemical change that takes place when earthenware is fired at extremely high temperatures. Stone can also refer to encaustic tiles **(inset)**, which are made of natural stone ground up with marble dust, which adds strength. Encaustic tiles are often patterned, and the pattern runs through the tile, which is an advantage if the tile becomes chipped. Because they are porous, all of these types of stone need sealing, but their advantage lies in the wide range of colours they offer and their mellow, ageless quality.

Terracotta tiles are made from low-fired red clay; **quarry tiles** from unrefined aluminium clay with a high silica content, and are high fired and therefore less porous. Both come in warm natural shades, and their resistance to water and grease makes them ideal in kitchens and hallways, although again they are cold underfoot. Prices vary, but it can be an inexpensive hard flooring choice, unless you choose reclaimed antique terracotta. Quarry tiles are the cheaper option.

25

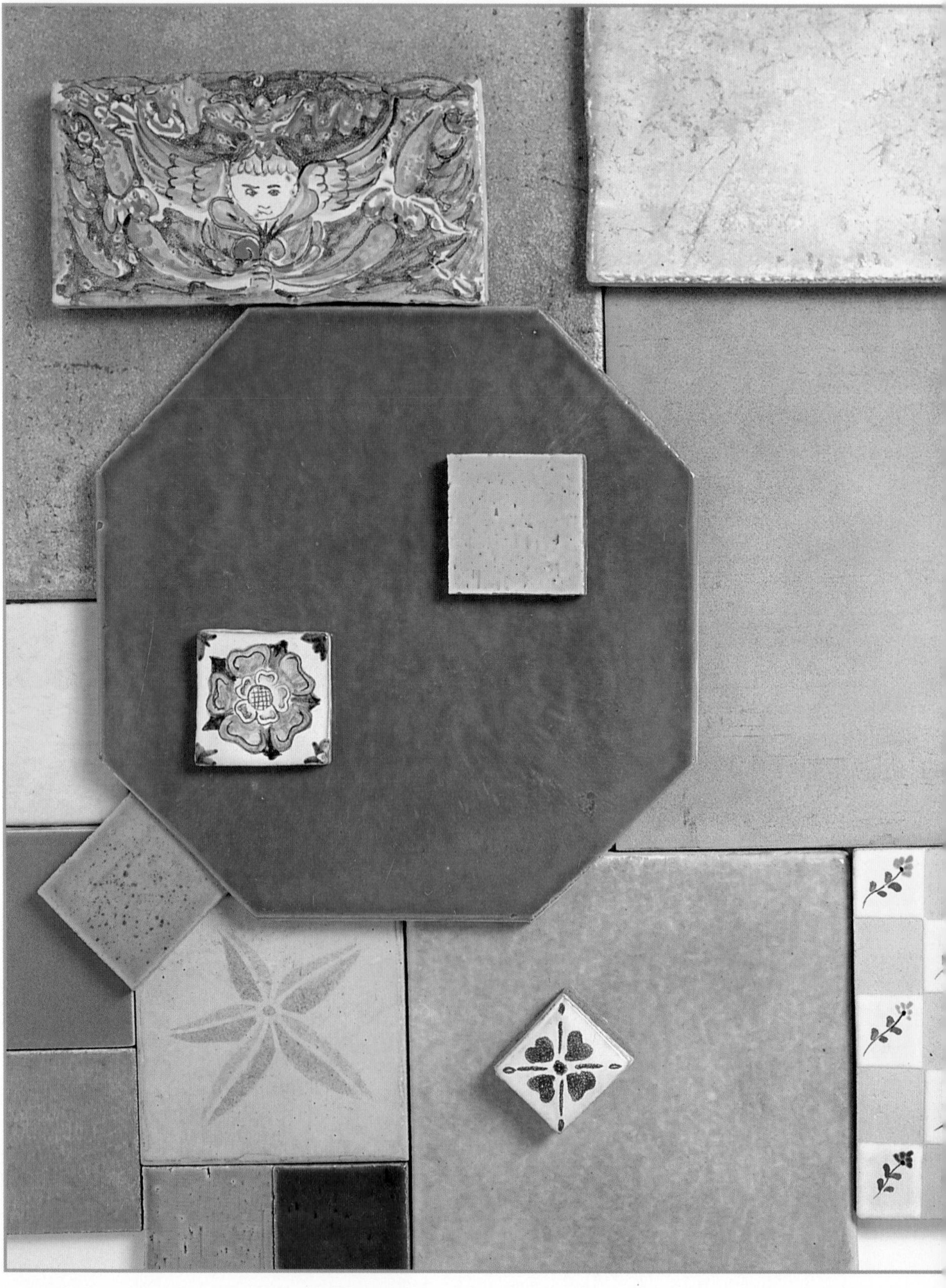

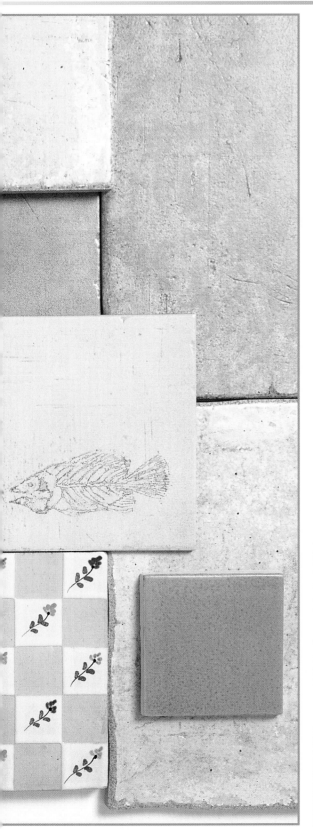

Ceramic tiles (left) are made from baked clay, and although they are the cheapest hard-floor option, they can wear; the glazed variety can also become slippery underfoot. The wide range of patterns and shapes makes them popular from a design point of view, and they are easy to keep clean, with no sealing or maintenance necessary.

Mosaic tiles (below) are not as exotic as they sound. They are made up of various materials, including marble, clay and glass silica, and can be bought in panels to make laying easier. They work well when inset into quarry-tiled floors, which will help to keep the cost down and is a fun way to experiment with pattern. No maintenance is necessary, but mosaic tiles can be very expensive if used on their own over large areas.

CARING FOR HARD FLOORS

Natural stone, like all floor coverings, needs care if it is to keep its appearance. Neglect or the wrong cleaning regime can actually be detrimental to the patina of the stone. Treat it like hardwood and you can't go wrong: stone does not like abrasives, bleach or domestic detergents, as the whitening additives lodge themselves in the pores of the stone and leave a film. Use products recommended by the manufacturer (some tile companies produce their own). Natural stone in a kitchen, where sealants and polishes will protect against splashes of oil and grease, will require a little more care. Ask your supplier to recommend the most suitable products.

Although laying most types of flooring is beyond the capabilities of most amateurs, quarry or ceramic tiles are simple enough to put down. These tiles are ideal for areas that may well be subject to water splashes, such as bathrooms, but check the floor is strong enough if you plan to lay them on floors above ground level.

The surface they lie on must be rigid, flat, dry and clean, and the floor well ventilated. See the drawing on page 40 for the technique of strengthening a floor with timber. If you are laying quarry tiles on chipboard, use a heavy-duty ceramic tile adhesive. On a solid concrete floor, use a 3:1 sand and cement screed.

To calculate the quantity of tiles you will need, measure the length and then the width of the room using the dimensions of the tile (adding on the width of the grouted join in between each tile) as one measuring unit. Round up both measurements to the nearest tile, then multiply the two figures together to give you the total number of tiles you need. Alternatively, if tiles come in packs, calculate the floor area of the room by measuring the width and the length and multiplying the two together. Then work out the number of packs you will need, using the coverage specified on each pack as a guide. If your room is an odd shape, divide it into smaller units and take measurements in the same way.

Note: Always allow for damaged tiles and breakage. It is better to have too many tiles than too few.

Method

Find the middle of the room by running string from the mid-point of one wall to the mid-point of the opposite wall, then repeat for the two remaining walls; the point at which the strings cross is the centre of the room. Lay your tiles down dry, in a line from the middle of the room to the wall, and then along the wall into the furthest corner from the door. Arrange the tiles so that at least half a tile-width is left around the edge of the room, then take two battens and lay them at 90 degrees to each other, placing them along the last complete row of tiles at the corner of the room. Nail the battens temporarily in place. Your starting point for tiling is at the corner where the battens meet.

Note: Tiling will raise the level of the floor so you may have to plane off the bottoms of doors.

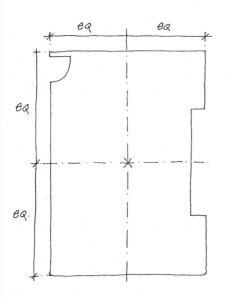
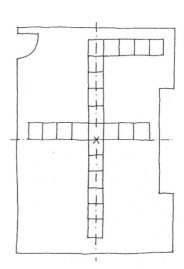
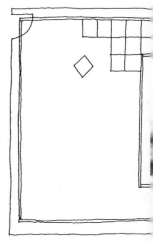

ou will need:

aterials
es
commended adhesive
wel
tched spreader
ing
irit level
oden battens
mmer and nails
e spacers
e cutter
onge
ut
an cloths
ber gloves
 hammer and pincers

If necessary, remove the irting boards and dry tile the m, fixing the battens in place outlined opposite.

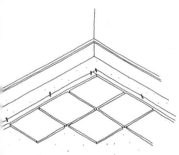

Remove the tiles, and using a wel and notched spreader, lay a d of adhesive over an area about square. You may need to apply hesive to the tiles as well. low the manufacturer's tructions.

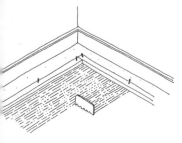

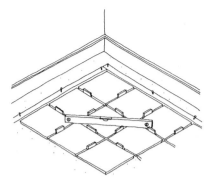

3. Place the tiles on the floor, twisting them slightly to increase the adhesion, then straighten them. Insert spacers before laying the next tile to maintain an even gap for grout. Work towards the door.

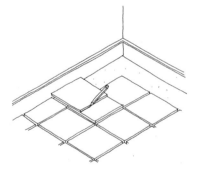

4. Check with a spirit level as you go along to make sure that the tiles are lying flat. Once all the whole tiles are laid leave them for 24 hours to ensure the adhesive is dry. Remove the battens.
5. Lay the edge tiles. Mark each tile to be cut by laying it over the last whole tile in the row, covering it exactly. Place another tile on top and push it against the wall over the gap. Draw a line where the top tile crosses the one below. Allow a margin for grouting. Cutting accurately will take a little practice; quarry tiles are

harder to cut than ceramic ones. If you are cutting awkward shapes, chip away at the back of the tile with a pin hammer (don't use the tile cutter), then turn the tile over and chip away at the front half. Finish off with pincers if necessary. It requires patience.

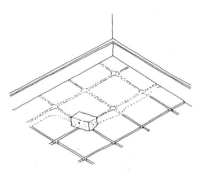

6. Use tile adhesive to fix any skirting tiles. Special round edged tiles make a neat job. Alternatively, replace the skirting board.
7. Once the adhesive has hardened (leave for at least 24 hours), use a sponge to apply grout between the tiles, working it into the joints and finishing flush with the tiles. Wipe off excess grout with a clean cloth.
8. Avoid heavy traffic on the tiles for 48 hours.
Note: tile grouts and adhesives vary. Always follow the manufacturer's instructions.

Laying tiles on screed

If you intend to lay tiles onto a concrete floor, it is better to set the tiles into a screed of sand and cement. This method is much more complicated than using adhesive, and it is recommended that you employ a professional craftsman so you can avoid expensive mistakes.

3 Semi-hard floors

Semi-hard flooring – cork tiles, rubber, linoleum, vinyl and natural matting – bridges the gap between hard, and often cold, natural flooring, and softer but not always practical carpeting. Semi-hard materials offer a solution where hard flooring is not suitable for the home for structural reasons, or where the budget will not stretch to the expense.

Softer floors are undoubtedly more economical – both in cost and in the time it takes to lay them and maintain them – and you will not need to sacrifice either quality or choice. The variety offered by this type of flooring has widened immeasurably since the days of the grey- or blue-speckled linoleum found in our mothers' kitchens. Colours, patterns and quality are now so good that in some cases you would be hard-pressed to tell at first glance whether the hall-way in the picture opposite was the real thing or a clever vinyl finish.

Types of semi-hard flooring

Cork (below) has been popular for years because it is a warm, soft, quiet surface to walk on and is surprisingly hard wearing and resilient. Some companies combine cork layers with wood on an MDF (medium-density-fibreboard) base, which makes it especially comfortable, and, as an added bonus, a good sound insulator. Cork has environmental advantages as well, because it is a renewable bark which is harvested every nine years and allowed to grow back again on the tree. The colour choice for cork has improved greatly, but it will need to be sealed with polyurethane, especially in a bathroom where water can seep into it. Yet it is still a relatively cheap floor covering, and most economical when you lay thinner tiles with adhesive onto hardboard. Always check you have flooring grade cork.

Rubber (above and left) **and linoleum** (below) **are both attractive and easy to clean.**

Rubber flooring is usually seen on the floors of health clubs or shops but now it is available in a wider range of colours, plain, patterned or textured – it looks very good with contemporary furnishings. Its non-slip qualities also make it ideal for a bathroom floor or an area near an outside doorway. If you want to mix it with a different flooring material, lay it next to varnished wood where the contrast of smooth and textured works very well. Rubber flooring comes in sheet or tile form, and can be laid with adhesive on screed concrete or a smooth, even sub-floor.

Linoleum was a name coined in 1863 and derives from the Latin words for oil and flax. It has environmental advantages because it is made from linseed oil, wood flour (finely ground wood), pine resin and natural pigments, which are baked slowly at high temperatures and pressed onto a jute backing. The linoleum that is available today is very hard wearing, not brittle and thin as it was in the 1940s and '50s, but flexible, very strong and warm underfoot. Linoleum comes in sheet or tile form, in a wide range of colours. Patterns can be created by hand- or aqua-jet-cutting, for which you may well need professional help. Manhandling large rolls of linoleum may make the job a bit daunting too. Otherwise it can be laid with the recommended adhesive onto a dry, even floor. Put in a damp-proof course if the flooring is at ground level. Linoleum can be swept, washed and polished with emulsion polish, but avoid strong alkaline cleaning agents. Don't let water get underneath as it will lift the linoleum. There are special paints that will renew a worn-out linoleum surface.

Vinyl is even more versatile than linoleum, but although the two seem similar they are in fact completely different. Vinyl (or polyvinyl chloride, PVC) is manufactured using chemicals, and is available as tiles or sheets up to 4m wide, in an enormous number of thicknesses and patterns. The fact that vinyl is used in public places such as shops, where hundreds of feet march over it, should tell you just how hard wearing and resistant it is as a flooring material: it is waterproof, resistant to oil and fat (but not to burns and grit abrasions) and easy to keep clean, so it should be able to withstand the wear-and-tear of the average family. **Cushioned vinyl** is backed with foam and has a 'blown' vinyl base, which holds the pattern, covered with a thick transparent layer. Its softness means it is comfortable underfoot. **Luxury vinyl tiles**, backed with recycled vinyl waste and with a thicker surface layer, are the top of the range and come in very convincing imitations of marble, timber, terracotta, stone or ceramic. Vinyl is valuable in small areas such as bathrooms, as it can be cut around awkward shapes.(See page 35 for details of how to do this.)

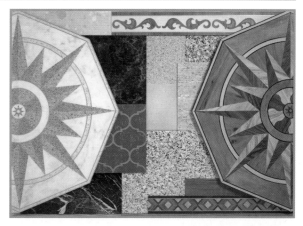

The sheer variety of colours and patterns available in vinyl, matched with its resilience and ease of care, make it a very good choice for kitchens, bathrooms and hallways.

33

Natural matting is categorised as semi-hard flooring because, while it is rather similar to carpeting, it does not have the cushioned soft quality of thick carpet. What natural fibres such as coir and sisal do offer, however, is a reasonably priced floor covering in beautiful natural colours, with developments over the years making it more hard wearing and dust resistant. It is also very fashionable now and its neutral appearance works well when linking rooms together, especially if the matting is broken up with the odd kilim or rug. Alternatively, it could be used as a mat over timber flooring or vinyl. Although it is a bit hard underfoot, it is suitable for a bedroom if a soft mat is placed beside the bed to ease early morning rising.

Sisal is produced from the leaves of the agave sisal, which grows in a sub-tropical climate, and is woven into a large variety of designs, such as herringbone and plaid. It is very hard wearing and is even suitable on stairs if it is fitted correctly with underlay. However, it should be treated with a stain resisting product. **Coir** comes from the husk of a coconut and is most often seen as door matting. In matting or tile form, it makes an extremely economical covering for a floor, although it is inclined to be prickly underfoot. You will need to touch and feel the varieties and weaves available to decide whether it is suitable for your needs.

Natural matting comes from a renewable source, so has an environmental appeal. It is also thought that its non-oiliness tends to stop it being a breeding ground for the bacteria that cause allergies. Jute and seagrass are other, similar natural matting materials, and all types are easy for a professional to lay.
Note: These floor coverings should not be used in a kitchen close to a cooker or sink, or in a living room near an open fire.

The soft colours of natural floor coverings such as sisal, coir and jute look very effective with modern furniture and furnishings. New developments have made them softer but more hard wearing and it is still an economical way to cover a floor.

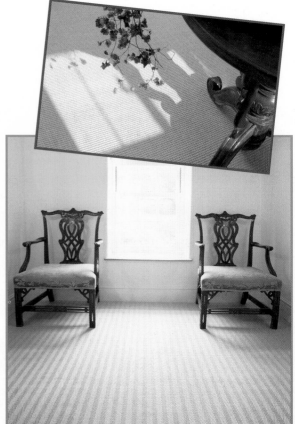

If you are feeling brave you could attempt to lay vinyl or linoleum in sheet form in a large area, but the sheer bulk of it can be daunting, so getting professional help might be wiser. Also, complicated pattern making, especially with linoleum, will very likely need to be done by a professional to avoid expensive mistakes.

Laying sheet flooring in a small bathroom or utility room is much easier, however, if you make a template out of paper cut to the shape of the whole floor, which makes cutting around obstacles such as a lavatory much easier.

You will need:

Materials
stiff paper
pencil
a small block of wood (about 4cm wide)
a very sharp Stanley knife

1. Lay the paper on the floor, temporarily fix with masking tape and then trim about 1cm in around the edges. It may help, with difficult obstacles such as lavatories, to make the template in two halves.
2. Holding the block of wood against the wall or shaped fitting, trace a pencil line onto the paper as you move around the room.
3. Lift the template and place it over the sheet flooring, taping it into place. Place one edge of the wooden block against the pencil line on the template and draw a pencil line onto the sheet flooring, using the outer edge of the block as your guide. The flooring can then be cut. When laying sheet flooring behind a lavatory you will need to make a cut at the back.

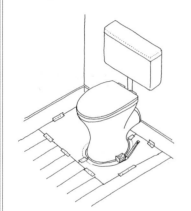
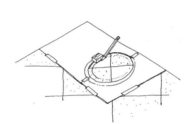
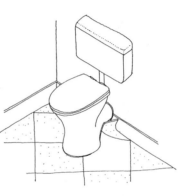

CARE AND MAINTENANCE OF SEMI-HARD FLOORS

Keep vinyl clean with warm soapy water, rinsing it off thoroughly. Avoid strong detergents, white spirit or turpentine, and wax polish – there are polishes that are especially recommended for these floors. Vinyl can be damaged by grit and burns, so if you are using vinyl tiles, keep some extra ones to replace any that become damaged. Slight scratches in the vinyl can be covered up by rubbing in a matching colour of shoe polish with cotton wool. Remove the excess with a cotton wool bud previously dampened with a little white spirit. Finish by polishing with a soft, clean cloth.

Linoleum can also be damaged by strong detergents, but sweeping and washing with a gentle cleaning product will maintain its appearance. Shine with emulsion polish or recommended polishes.

Rubber can be cleaned with mild detergents and even disinfected with well-diluted disinfectant. Make sure grime does not build up around textured finishes.

Natural floor coverings should be cleaned with a vacuum cleaner. Those without a backing should have the occasional sweep underneath. Stains should be dealt with promptly; a proprietary treatment is available from manufacturers for use on natural fibres. For best results, all natural flooring material should be laid out in the room for 48 hours before it is installed so it can acclimatise to the atmosphere.

Note: With all detergents and cleaning products, check the manufacturer's notes about their suitability for use on certain surfaces, and always follow the instructions carefully.

4 Wooden floors

Wood has a warmth of colour, and a warmth underfoot, which makes it a wonderful choice for flooring. It is hard wearing and improves with age. It is easy to keep clean, which makes it ideal for allergy sufferers, and offers incredible versatility in what you can do with it: varnish it, sand it, stencil it, stain it, even create patterns with it.

The naturalness of wood is its great appeal. While so many materials are now manufactured and therefore uniform in appearance, it is the imperfections, the knots and the variety in colour, that make every wooden floor unique. Wood is the best choice of flooring to partner with stone, vinyl or linoleum. It can be covered with rugs, and will show off their patterns to the best effect. It is an excellent background, too, for decorating around, whether your style is simple or flamboyant.

Wood is an economical choice (so long as you're careful which timber you choose to lay), because a little inspiration will transform even the most run-of-the-mill timber. If you live in an older property, there may well be a substantial hardwood floor in place beneath the existing floor covering.

Types of wooden flooring

Hardwood boards, such as oak, ash, walnut, elm and maple, have the greatest durability, and the deepest warmth of colour, but as a result are the most expensive. Pine, a **softwood**, is cheaper and less interesting on the eye, but lends itself to staining or painting. Hardwoods are also less appealing from an environmental point of view, unless they come from managed forests, whereas pine is a readily renewable source.

Wooden flooring, with its wonderful variety in tone, is warm in colour and underfoot.

Wooden flooring comes in a variety of forms: boards of varying widths, ready-made strips and short pieces of hardwood used for parquet, tiles and panels (often pre-sealed veneered softwood), and blocks. Look for reputable suppliers who can show you what is available. They may well supply some more exotic woods, such as purple heart or willow, which make wonderfully interesting flooring. They should also be able to advise on the best woods to suit your property and your budget.

All wooden flooring should be sealed; take advice on the products that are most suitable for your chosen timber, as the products available improve every year. As an alternative, timber – especially hardwood – can be polished deeply and regularly. This will bring out the patina of the wood better than any other treatment.

Left: **Wood makes a good play surface and** (inset) **highly polished, good quality floorboards such as these make an excellent backdrop for the intricate design and rich colours of this drawing room rug.**

Manufactured woods are the most economical option, especially when used in sheet form over poor quality floorboards. These timbers – chipboard, hardboard and plywood, all of which are manufactured materials – can look very stylish when finished with paint, stain or varnish. But however you choose to treat them, manufactured woods are not as hard wearing as the natural material and will need sealing.

Timber-faced plywood can be bought as tongue-and-groove and laid like any other wood. Condition the timber by leaving it out for 48 hours in the room in which it will be laid. A poor quality or weak floor can be strengthened with an overlay of wooden sheeting.

STRENGTHENING A FLOOR WITH WOODEN SHEETING

1. Lay the sheets with their lengths at right angles to the direction of the floorboards.
2. Stagger the joints between the sheets like brickwork, and nail them down at 15cm intervals, using gripping nails to prevent them pulling loose as the floor flexes.
3. The nails should be hammered in flush with the level of the floor to stop them snagging rugs or feet.

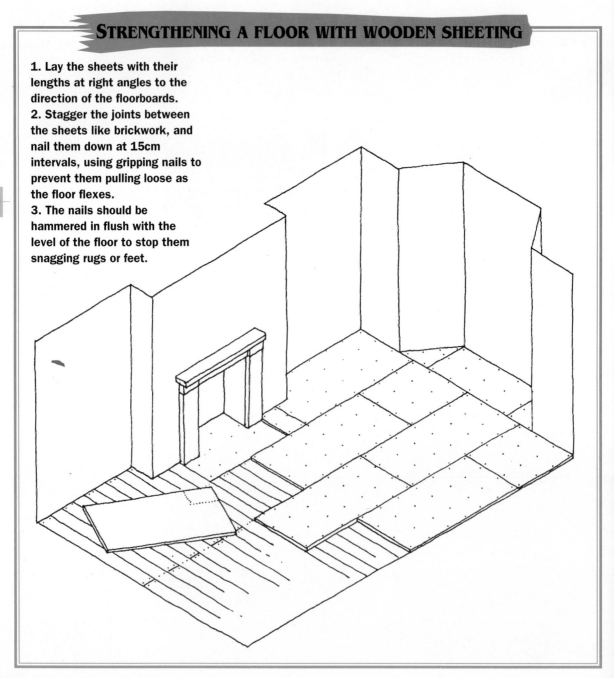

40

Laying a wooden floor

Once you have chosen the right type and quality of wooden floor, it must be properly dried and seasoned. Too much haste when laying wooden floors can result in disaster. As wood is a 'living' material it will react to its environment, either shrinking or expanding, depending on the conditions. The moisture content needs to suit that of the room (less moisture content for underfloor heating, more for central heating – ask your supplier). To be sure that no major changes will occur, lay the wood out in the room it will be installed in for 48 hours so that it can acclimatise.

Boards can be nailed straight into existing joists, tongue-and-groove boards snapping together easily (once you have had a bit of practice!), but the biggest mistake most people make is to miss the joists and nail though water pipes or electric cables. Before you start, make a 'map' of the floor, marking where these services are located. Parquet or wood strip should be laid onto hardboard or plywood that is absolutely level. Wood block and wood mosaic floors should be laid on a concrete screed or onto plywood, and fixed with adhesive or discreet nailing.

Mosaic tiles are blocks manufactured in a criss-cross pattern. They are supplied sanded and sealed in a pack of panels, and are designed to be easy to lay.

You will need:

Materials
wooden mosaic tiles
recommended adhesive
notched spreader
warm water and clean cloths
trimming knife
fine-toothed tenon saw
piece of cardboard or profile gauge

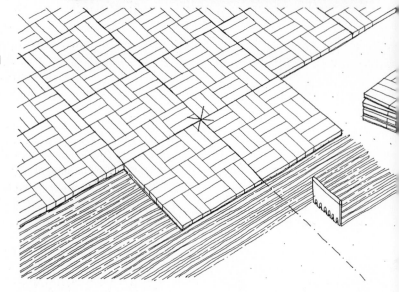

1. Ensure that the surface is completely dry, clean and level. If you are laying a hardboard floor underneath, follow the instructions on page 40 for laying this type of flooring.

2. Gauge the centre of the room using the same technique outlined on page 28. Dry lay the mosaic tiles from this point to the walls, but you will need to adjust the starting point if there is less than half a tile-width at the wall. Leave a small gap at each edge of the room for the tiles to expand.

3. Lay tiles from the centre outwards, using a notched spreader to spread the adhesive. Work a small area at a time, because the adhesive dries in about 20 minutes; as the tiles are flexible, practise laying them down on a dry area of floor first. A bowl of warm water and a cloth kept close at hand will be useful for wiping off adhesive that gets onto the tiles.

4. When you reach the edges you will need to trim the tiles to fit. Measure out how wide the edging tile must be, using the same technique as on page 28 for laying ceramic and quarry tiles. Cut the back of the tile between the wooden strips with a trimming knife, or, if you are cutting across the strips, use a fine-toothed tenon saw, cutting with the face of the tile upwards.

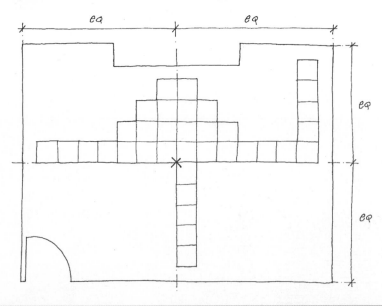

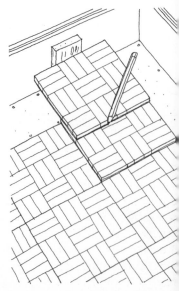

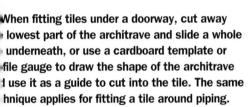

When fitting tiles under a doorway, cut away
lowest part of the architrave and slide a whole
underneath, or use a cardboard template or
file gauge to draw the shape of the architrave
and use it as a guide to cut into the tile. The same
technique applies for fitting a tile around piping.

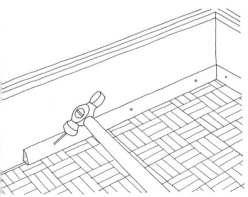

Once you have finished tiling cover the
expansion gap with timber mouldings pinned to
the skirting
If the tiles are not pre-sealed, leave for 2-3
weeks, then seal with the approved sealant,
using three or more coats.

You may be lucky enough to discover neglected but
serviceable floorboards under your floor covering,
which need only to be stripped, sanded and sealed,
or painted, stained or varnished.

Gaps between floorboards can be a problem. They
are dust traps and channel draughts. Fill them with
narrow strips of wood or wood filler. One resourceful
technique is to block the holes with old wine bottle
corks – not exactly conventional, but interesting!
The best solution, however, is to lift all the
floorboards with a claw hammer and shunt them
along, relaying them so they are flush with each
other, and then filling in the edge gaps with new,
narrow boards.

If shunting the boards is not necessary, check
that there are no protruding nails before you start
treating the boards. Run your hand, covered in a
'glove' of nylon tights or stocking, over the boards.
This will detect any protruding screws or nails.
Note: when lifting floorboards always turn off the
electricity supply in case you encounter a cable.

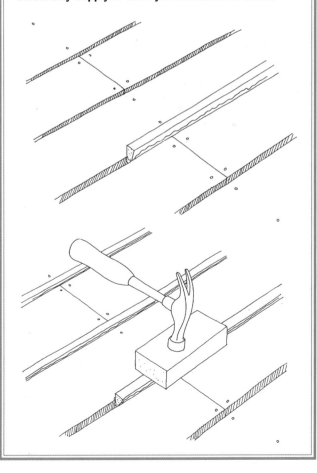

Once the boards are made good, and rotten ones have been replaced, you will be able to sand the floor; this will take off the top surface of the boards, cleaning and lightening them. Hire a belt sander for the job, but follow the instructions carefully. Although sanders vacuum up a certain amount of the dust, it is still important to wear protective clothing, a mask and eye protection, and to keep doors sealed and windows open at all times.

1. If the floorboards are cupped or ridged, or if you want to remove old paint, then sand diagonally across the boards at 45°. Then change to a medium abrasive and work at right angles to the first direction.
2. If you simply want to remove old polish, use a fine abrasive working along the boards in the direction of the grain.
3. Finish off the edges with a hand sander, again using less coarse abrasives as you work.
4. Leave overnight so the dust can settle, and then vacuum clean and wipe over with a clean rag dampened with white spirit. Then seal using a sealer recommended by your flooring specialist.

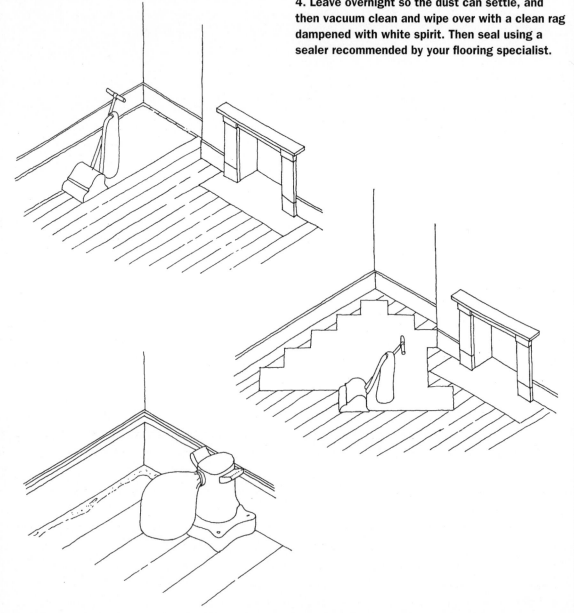

Finishes for wooden floors

Before treating your wooden floors with any finish, make sure they have been properly repaired (see page 43).

Liming (above left) can be done either with limed wax, white paint thinned with white spirit or turpentine, or gesso, mixed thin so it is runny. Paint your liming solution along the boards, working a length of about 90cm at a time, board by board, then wipe the paint off with a cleaning rag, working one way along the timber. Leaving paint in the cracks creates the desired effect. Leave to dry.

Staining (above right) leaves the grain of the wood showing through while adding colour and interest. It is particularly suitable where the floorboards are not in good enough condition to be varnished. Stain comes in a large variety of colours, including many natural wood shades, so you can create a marquetry effect, paint borders with contrasting colour to the rest of the floor, or stencil in natural tones for a really effective finish. Boards painted alternate wood tones look particularly good. Beech, a softwood, can be improved if stained in a soft greyish-white before sealing. Apply stain with a cloth, rubbing it over the wood so you are working with the boards, not against them. Colours can bleed, so use the edge of the board as a boundary for each colour, or, if you are working across the timber, score a shallow line with a Stanley knife, which will also work as a boundary. Some stains include a sealant: others will need sealing. Select the right product for the right stain.

Varnish, like stain, comes in a variety of colours, but leaves an appealing finish whether you use matt or gloss. It takes patience to apply, but more importantly, it is imperative the floor is absolutely clean and dust-free before application.

Paint will transform boards that are not attractive enough to be left plain. The floor works as a canvas, which offers versatility, but if it is your first attempt at painting floors, don't be too ambitious. Alternate geometric patterns are simple, and look very effective. For old boards, apply a coat of diluted acrylic wood primer, one part primer to one part water, then apply a coat of undiluted primer. For new floorboards, apply a coat of PVA sealer, sand the floor, and then apply one coat of acrylic wood primer. Chipboard and hardboard should also be treated with PVA sealer, adding a layer of emulsion to the chipboard.

Once you have prepared the floor, you can then apply the paint. Floors can simply be painted with emulsion and several coats of protective varnish, but plan carefully if you want to create a pattern, as it will be difficult to live with if you get it wrong. To create a pattern, first apply a coat of emulsion. If you want a diamond or check pattern, or even stencilled borders around the edge of the wooden floor, measure carefully so the pattern is symmetrical; mark the squares with faint pencil marks, or use a paper template. Once the paint is dry and the design complete, seal the floor with two or three coats of clear water-based floor varnish, more if the floor will have to cope with heavy traffic. Polyurethane varnish is more hard wearing but harder to apply, and takes longer to dry. Ask your supplier to recommend the most suitable product.

TIP

- **Marine paint is very durable, but takes a long time to dry, and the colour choice is not very wide.**
- **Always work towards the door. If you don't, you won't be the first who has been stuck on the wrong side of a room with a newly-painted floor!**

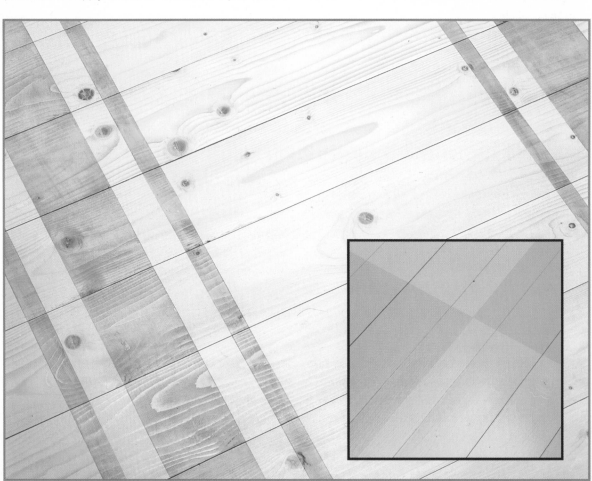

Find inspiration by copying designs from books and textiles, without being over-ambitious if you are a beginner. You might want to try one of the following.

• A lattice pattern with squares and rectangles, highlighting each crossing point with a contrasting coloured diamond.

• A 3-D marquetry effect, achieved with darker colours and a stencilled central pattern.

• A fake kilim, made either with home-made stencils or pre-cut patterns. Plan the design carefully on paper first, and measure out where the designs will fall.

• A simple freehand floral design in a small space such as a bathroom or child's room. Pick an existing design in the room as a motif. Keep the images simple, even naive.

• Borders with leaf patterns, waving lines or a sprigged pattern. 'Enclose' the border with a straight painted line. Keep the line straight using masking tape as a guide.

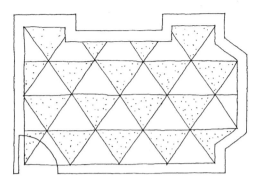

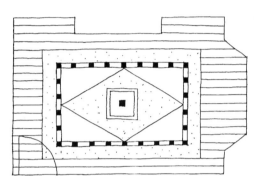

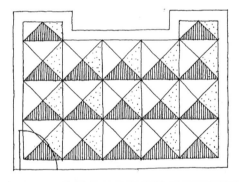

CARE AND MAINTENANCE OF WOODEN FLOORING

All timber floors, whether stained, painted, varnished or left natural, need to be sealed with the recommended sealant. Ask you supplier's advice on what to use, and be careful to choose a clear varnish if you don't want to affect the colour underneath. Once stains wear, the floor will need to be re-sanded, and the whole process carried out from scratch for a uniform finish. However, where there are only a few worn areas, if care is taken, it is possible to sand a painted floor in these areas only, and reapply the paint with the correct finish without having to tackle the whole floor.

Wood can be swept, and wiped with a damp (but not soaking) cloth or mop, rather than scrubbed. Polish, which is time-consuming to apply, creates a wonderful result on old timbers, although it can be slippery. Fix rugs to polished floors using special sticky rug underlay or tape, available from carpet suppliers (see Chapter 5).

5 Carpets and rugs

There is no floor surface that compares to the softness underfoot of a carpet or rug. While we look for practicality in the rooms that demand it, most of us choose comfort in the rooms where we want to relax. But carpets and rugs do more than just cushion our tread. They are an excellent insulator, and therefore make sound economic sense in a country where we have more cold months than warm ones in the year. Carpets and rugs also play a large part in the decoration of a room.

We will deal with rugs later in this chapter, concentrating here on how to make the right colour choice for a carpet, which is after all a far more permanent fixture than a rug.

Choosing the right colour

A plain coloured carpet makes up a very large visual area of a room. Choose the right colour for your carpet and it will work like a canvas, bringing together the patterns and tones of the rest of the room. Colour can also help to deceive the eye. As a rule, the darker the colour the smaller a room will look – not always the answer if you are not overwhelmed with space. With a small room you would be better to choose paler shades, and make up for what you have lost in the practicality of darker colours by choosing a carpet that is more stain resistant and harder wearing. The reverse, of course, is also true, that darker colours will help to diminish a larger space (darker colours always seem closer to the eye), and can make a cool, rather impersonal large room seem cosier. A warning about the practicality of darker colours however. They may not show mud or dirt, but while light-coloured specks seem to disappear into paler coloured carpets, they show up as clear as day on darker shades. It's a question of balancing the pros and cons.

Warm colours are found in the oranges, apricots, terracottas, ochres and soft pinks. These particularly suit rooms that are naturally quite dark; they make them feel cosier.

Neutral colours include beige, white, cream and straw. These colours provide light and space, and are a good foil for very strong colours in furnishing fabrics and paintwork.

Cool colours are the blues, greens and pale yellows. These work well in bright sunny rooms, but may need warming colours close to them in darker situations.

A carpet can play a leading role in the room if you choose one with a contemporary pattern – geometric or with small motifs. These are more subtle and less overpowering than the swirly designs of the 1960s and '70s, and it is generally the colour which dominates anyway. Patterned or flecked carpets are ideal for hallways or children's rooms because they don't show the dirt.

It's worth considering a border when planning your carpeting. A border of a contrasting pattern or colour can look very effective around the edge of a room, especially in larger rooms where the border will 'bring in' the walls. Borders are also effective up the side of a stair carpet. The result is a happy compromise between a block of solid colour on the floor and a more dominating pattern.

Your local carpet supplier will recommend an expert carpet fitter to lay the border correctly. It is too complicated for an amateur to tackle.

51

Contemporary patterned carpets are available in subtler designs these days and add interest where a room is plain or needs some warmth. Even ethnic kilim designs can be found in Axminster weave carpets. As a rule, the smaller the room the smaller the pattern should be, or it will dominate everything. A carpet with a pattern of appropriate size will unite the colour scheme of the paint and soft furnishings.

e texture and colour of the carpet can change the whole character of a room. Soft, pale ours may be the least practical, but they make a good background for the details and fabrics ed in the rest of the room.

Carpet fibres

Broadly speaking, carpets are made from wool, synthetic fibres or from a combination of both. Prices vary as much as the colour choice or quality, between £2 and £100 per square metre, but if you make an informed choice about the right carpet for the right situation you could get quite a bargain for a floor covering that can last for 15 years or more. In fact market research has shown that only one-third of carpet buyers were replacing them because they had worn out. The large majority were replacing perfectly serviceable carpets because the colour or pattern had gone out of fashion or they wanted to redecorate the room.

Once you have worked out how many square metres of carpet you will need (by taking the length and the width measurement of the room and multiplying the two together) add 50 per cent again for underlay, grippers and fitting. Some carpet companies offer free fitting or underlay, but look carefully because the price of these will be hidden somewhere, and you may be sacrificing the quality of the carpet for what seems to be a good bargain.

100% wool carpets, usually using wool from Britain or New Zealand, are the softest and most luxurious, with the deepest colour quality. They are also the most robust. Because wool is a natural product it resists dirt and is easy to look after and keep clean; it bounces back after it has been crushed (by the legs of furniture especially); it is fairly fire retardent, and resists static build-up because of its ability to hold moisture. Yet all this comes at a price of course. Furthermore, wool is not a very good choice in a bathroom exactly because of its ability to retain moisture, and it will tend to smell musty if it becomes too wet. **80% wool/20% nylon** is a more popular choice because it combines all the advantages of a natural and a synthetic material with less expense. The nylon woven into the carpet lends an added resilience, while still being static-free and very soft underfoot.

The following fibres often appear in carpets blended with other materials, either natural or manufactured.
Nylon is the most frequently used manufactured fibre for carpeting. It is very good value, and is soft and resilient, wearing well, but nylon can stain easily unless it is treated first, and it is inclined to trap dust and dirt.
Polypropylene is also a cheap carpet option, and has the advantage of being hard wearing and resilient. Its softness and fluffiness, combined with its moisture and stain resistance, makes it an ideal choice for bathrooms, but it does tend to flatten easily and its thickness can make it hard work to vacuum. These disadvantages often disappear when polypropylene appears in a wool blend.

Polyester is also used in bathrooms and bedrooms because it is bulky and soft, but only relatively hard wearing. Polyester is easy to look after and economical too, but is not colourfast.

Acrylic is also a cheap option, and although it performs like wool, it is not usually fire retardent (although this can vary in degree) and it flattens and stains more easily, although stains are easy to remove.

Blends obviously aim to provide the best of all worlds. A new wool, nylon and polyester mixture produces a durable carpet which does not shed fibres, as wool can do, and is less likely to pull. Blends improve all the time, so it is best to shop around and ask your supplier about new products on the market.

Axminster (left) **is the top of the range weave for patterned carpets where the pattern is interwoven. A cheaper option is a tufted weave with a printed design.**

When choosing a carpet, the way it feels will be your best guide, but technically there are two distinct types of carpet construction: woven and tufted.

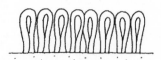

Woven carpet is the finest quality. The pile and the jute- or cotton-backing materials are closely interwoven using Axminster (see previous page) or Wilton machinery, which give these carpets their names. The result is a highly dense carpet, the Wilton method using more yarn than the Axminster, which makes it more expensive. Wilton carpets tend to be plain or have only simple patterns; Axminsters lend themselves to more detailed designs – in fact the name Axminster is sometimes synonymous in people's minds with heavily patterned carpets.

Tufted carpets have pile that is stitched into a pre-woven backing, then secured with a layer of latex and strengthened with jute, polypropylene or foam. The basic carpets are usually plain; patterns are put on mechanically or by printing. Examples of tufted weave carpets include:
loop pile, where the yarn forms a loop into the carpet backing, resulting in a soft, even pile (often seen on Berber carpets);

velvet, which has a very short pile that has been cut and then sheared to make a smooth and soft finish;
twist, whereby loops have been cut and the tufts twisted and then heat-set to make them more resistant to shading (flattening) or fluffing; and
saxony, which has a long thick cut with a soft, often textured appearance.

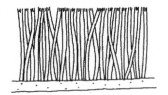

   Shorter piles are more suited to areas where there is a lot of traffic over the carpet. Longer piles are more luxurious, but better suited to a bedroom or bathroom. Loop piles are more resilient, whereas cut pile may show the indentation of furniture.

Right carpet, right place

The variety in quality and fibres in a carpet make them more or less suitable for certain rooms and positions in the house. It is important to get the quality right because an unresilient carpet in a hallway or an over-expensive one in a bedroom will be a waste of money in the long run.

Kitchens do not really suit carpeting because there is a high risk of spills, but you may be able to use a very short pile carpet that is stain resistant and easy to wipe clean. Carpet tiles are another idea because you can lift a tile that has witnessed a disaster and swap it with a clean one from a less obvious place in the room.

Bathrooms have the same problems as a kitchen, where moisture can be the biggest hazard, but there is a certain luxury, on a cold morning, in walking barefoot on a carpeted floor. If you do choose carpet, the backing needs to be waterproof, especially in smaller rooms, and you will have to make sure the ventilation is adequate. Hessian-backed carpet may be suitable in a larger bathroom, but it is recommended that you use a large bath mat and a shaped, washable mat around the lavatory. Cotton carpet, which is quite new on the market, would be a possible solution.

Bedrooms are the obvious place for carpeting. Traffic is usually minimal, so you may be able to save money on quality, and a longer pile will give a more luxurious feel underfoot. For children's rooms, a stain resistant, easy to clean, shorter pile carpet would be a better choice.

Living rooms, including the dining room, need hard wearing varieties and, where food and drink is consumed, a degree of stain resistance. The quality of the carpeting and the depth of colour should be as good as the other furnishings in the room so the overall effect is not spoiled.

Hallways and landings, where traffic is at its heaviest, need strong, short pile carpeting, of the best quality that you can afford. Protect areas of heaviest use (just inside doorways for example) with rugs or with an extra piece of carpet in the same colour. The carpet you choose should be a practical colour and easy to vacuum clean.

Stairs take the worst treatment, so they need the hardest wearing carpeting with the most resilient underlay (felt being the best choice). Natural fibres are now more suitable than they once were for stairways. The stair carpet will start to show wear sooner than any other carpeting in the house, especially if the carpet is badly fitted, so make sure that it is utterly secure by using the correct gripper rods. It is a good idea to add an extra length of the carpet at the top and bottom of each flight so the carpet can be shifted periodically to even out wear. Ask your fitter the best way to do this. The edge of each tread must also be smooth so it does not snag the carpet, and loose timbers should be secured to minimise wear.

Stair rods, although purely decorative, give a wonderful finishing touch to a flight of stairs. Made from hardwood, brass and steel, they come with intricate inlays or finishes, many with witty finials. Remember to let the rods protrude at least 20cm either side of the carpet for the best effect.

Stair carpeting must be resilient, but it should also be in a warm and welcoming colour, and link the colour scheme of the entrance hall with the stairwell and upper floors. It can look most effective on stairs of stone or attractive timber, in which case the carpet should be narrower than the width of the tread. The exposed edges of timber stairs can then be painted – stencilled patterns making a pretty detail.

Underlay

Underlay is a very important part of laying a carpet, so don't imagine that just because it can't be seen it won't be needed. Not only does it act as a shock absorber, help minimise the indentation made by the legs of furniture, and insulate against noise, cold and dust coming up through floorboards, but it can also increase the life of the carpet by about 40 per cent. Even natural matting such as coir and sisal should have underlay. So, unless your carpet is foam backed, it must be included in your budget, but don't be fobbed off with special deals, or settle for the unspecified 'free underlay' mentioned in a quote (nothing is free, however it is presented to you). It is important to have the right underlay for the right carpet. There are various types to select from.

Felt, made from hair, wool jute and other natural and synthetic products, is dense and firm, has excellent insulation and is one of the cheapest.

Latex, a soft foam, is better for use in areas which have minimal traffic.

Rubber crumb is a blend of reconstituted rubber (car tyres) and latex emulsion; it is hard wearing enough for stairs and landings.

Waffle sponge rubber is soft and resilient and can be used almost universally.

When buying underlay remember these points:

• Don't try to save money by laying old underlay. It will have lost its resilience and the new carpet won't lie evenly.

• Look for the words 'British Standard BS5808 (1991)' on any underlay you buy.

• Compare prices, as some expensive underlays may just be marked up so that a particular carpet can be offered at a keener price.

• If your carpet is continuing into different rooms or throughout the house, use the same underlay (and the one most suitable for the heaviest use) under the whole area; this is likely to be the one most suitable for the stairs.

• Avoid felt if you have underfloor heating, as it will stop the heat from rising. Also, rubber crumb can sometimes smell when it is warm. Ask your supplier for advice.

• If your carpet is already foam backed, put down paper felt (which is like thin card) or newspaper as an underlay to stop the foam sticking to the floor underneath. Paper felt will also stop dust rising up through very gappy floorboards. It is not necessary on a concrete floor.

Buying and fitting a carpet

When you have thought through the practicalities and your preferences, gather together snippets of wallpaper, fabric samples and paint colours on a plain white piece of paper, and take this along with you to the carpet showroom. This will help you to whittle down the vast colour and pattern choices, although the decision about the weave and type of carpet will have shortened the long list of possibilities even further.

Bring all the possible samples together, because the one on the other side of the showroom that looked suitable at first glance will no doubt seem wrong when you place it alongside others under consideration. Once you have narrowed the field to three or four, ask for a sample of each to take home – any reputable dealer will allow this – and try the samples in both natural and artificial light. When you have made your choice, make a note of the instructions for caring for your chosen carpet.

Measuring up for a carpet can be complicated, especially on a staircase or narrow hallway, and while the very brave might try to calculate, order and lay their own carpeting, it is really best to use experts. Carpets are large, heavy and bulky, and need special tools to lay them correctly. Measuring is usually a free service, and experts will be able to calculate the amount of carpet you need with the minimum of wastage. A good carpet fitter will have only a small amount of carpet left over once the job is complete. If the carpet is being laid next to an outside door, ask them to allow for enough for an extra piece to use as a doormat. A carpet layer will also supply the underlay you have chosen and the gripper rods and junction rods where necessary. It is better to use metal or wood junctions on carpeting than to stitch it down, in case it should ever need to be lifted.

Before you pay for your carpet, check the following:

- Do you know what the price includes?
- Are you absolutely happy with the colour? You cannot change it once it is laid.
- Is the carpet you have chosen stain proof and easy to clean?
- Have you checked that a large roll of carpet can be taken into the room easily? This can be a problem with small upstairs rooms, where the only access may be through the window.
- Are you able to get rid of any old flooring your new carpet is replacing? Most carpet fitters will not be responsible for this.
- Will there be a charge for moving furniture, or for planing doors? Planing is a necessary job if the carpet is thicker than previous flooring.
- Is the carpet fitter insured for accidental damage?
- If you are concerned or need advice, contact the National Institute of Carpet and Floor Layers (0115 958 3077).

Rugs

The beauty of rugs lies in their versatility and their variety. Prices vary from a few pounds for small manufactured rugs, which often come in fun colours and prints suitable for a child's room, to thousands of pounds for handwoven ethnic rugs in silks and embroidery. Rugs can cover up a dull or cheap floor cover, enhance a beautiful hardwood floor, warm up a cold stone floor, or break the monotony of a top quality vinyl one. Rugs also make the surface a little softer underfoot. All this, and you can roll them up and take them with you when you move house!

Amateurs can come to grief when buying rugs of any value. If you are worried about whether you are making the right investment, buy because you like it and because it goes well in your home. You could also get a second opinion from another rug dealer. Cheaper copies of oriental designs manufactured in Europe (usually Belgium) are available, and although

they may not be equal in quality or colour tone, they are far cheaper than the real thing.

Rugs with patterns go against all the rules of interior design: even intricate designs can sit well with patterned furnishing fabrics, as long as the tones are right and the basic colours are co-ordinated. Obviously, strong geometric designs work better in simple modern situations, whereas floral Aubusson styles suit more traditional, delicate decor, but there are no hard and fast rules in between. Some contemporary rug makers will make a rug of your own design to order.

When buying a rug, keep the following in mind:
• Make sure the proportions and colours are right for the room; go to a showroom armed with measurements and swatches of fabric or paint colour used in the rest of the room. In most cases you will be able to take a rug home on trial to make sure it is right. Live with it for at least 24 hours so you see it in all lights.
• Make sure dyes are fast if it is to sit on top of a pale carpet.
• To spot a handwoven rug, turn it over and check that the fringing is a continuation of the weave. On manufactured rugs the fringing will have been sewn on.
• Handmade rugs will also have imperfections, and each one will be different from the next. This is part of their beauty.
• When buying an antique rug check the back for quality and neat knotting. Bend the back too. Cracking will mean the weave has dried out and is likely to rot.
• If the rug is to lie on a slippery floor surface attach a piece of non-slip underlay cut to size to the back of the mat. This will either be in the form of tacky matting or coated mesh. Likewise, mats that curl at the corners can be held flat with small grips, one side of which has a sticky surface which adheres to the underside of each corner of the rug, the other side gripping the carpet beneath with small metal hooks which work like cat's claws.

Rugs come in such a rich variety that there will always be one to fit your particular style and budget. Nothing can beat the quality of weave and colour in traditional rugs, especially oriental ones, but there are plenty of less expensive copies available. Kilims and modern geometric designs add fresh interest and a focal point for a room.

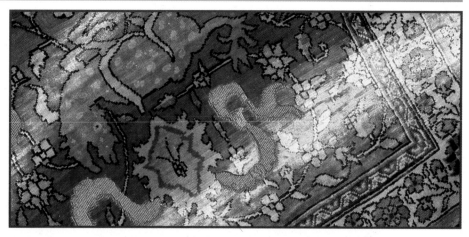

CARE AND MAINTENANCE OF CARPETS AND RUGS

There was once a widely-held belief that a new carpet should not be vacuumed for a while. This is nonsense. Dust builds up very quickly in carpeting, and you will be doing the carpet and yourself a favour by vacuuming often, right from the start. Carpets and rugs benefit most from regular vacuuming, once or twice a week, more if they are in heavy use. Lift rugs occasionally and vacuum the back. This will dislodge more ingrained dirt and dust. However, silk rugs should never be vacuumed; simply brush them with a soft brush in the direction of the pile. Rugs should not be beaten – it is a common myth that they should be – because it can damage the pile, and they should be turned regularly if they lie in direct sunlight, to minimise fading.

All carpets (not rugs) benefit from a wet clean, depending on how heavily they are used. Although carpet cleaning machines are available for hire, professional carpet cleaning companies have more up-to-date and efficient equipment, and will often move heavy furniture where

necessary. Your local carpet dealer may be able to recommend a cleaning company, but there is a trade association, The National Carpet Cleaners Association (0116 2543552), who will be able to give you a list of members in your area. Allow the carpet to dry completely after treatment, and use plastic or glass caster cups under metal casters to avoid rusting, which will mark the carpet.

Dry powder cleaners work well as a quick freshening-up method – to cover up pet smells for example – for some people they can be irritating to the skin. Make sure there is good ventilation by opening windows where possible, and empty the vacuum cleaner bag once you have finished vacuuming up the powder.

Stains can be a problem with carpets and rugs, and even stain-proofing will not make a carpet completely infallible, although it is a good idea as a specification when buying a carpet. Stains should be dealt with quickly using the correct treatment to prevent the stain becoming permanent.

• Animal and baby accidents, beer, wine, chocolate and fruit juices should be mopped with undyed absorbent paper (such as kitchen paper) as quickly as possible to stop the substance getting into the pile. Then wash gently with well-diluted detergent (the type used for washing woollens) or carpet shampoo according to the manufacturer's instructions. Rinse, and rub the carpet gently with a clean cloth in the direction of the pile.

• Paint must not be allowed to dry. Scrape off the excess with a spatula or knife, then, in the case of emulsion, gently clean as above. Oil-based paint will need to be dabbed first with white spirit or turpentine using a clean, undyed cloth.

• Scorch marks on carpets may need rubbing gently with sand paper to remove the scorched fibre tips.

Warning: certain products such as white spirit or nail varnish remover can damage a carpet if used in excess. It is often advisable to seek professional advice before starting to tackle such a stain.

63

Acknowledgements

The author and publishers are grateful to the following companies for permission to use photographs of their products in this book:

The Amtico Company (0171 629 6258) on pages 14, 16, 33.

Charterhouse Conservatories (01705 504006) on page 12.

Crucial Trading Ltd (01588 673666) on page 34.

Dalsouple rubber flooring (available from First Floor 0171 736 1123 or Millers 0131 554 2408) on page 32.

Decorwool (01943 603888) on pages 13, 48, 50, 57.

Fired Earth (01295 812 088) for your nearest stockist: rugs, natural flooring and matting on pages 11, 15, 20, 22, 24, 34, 60.

Junckers (01376 517512 for stockists) on pages 18, 38, 41.

Paris Ceramics (0171 371 7778 or 01423 523877) on page 21.

Waxman Ceramics of Elland (01422 311331) on page 27.

Wellington Tile Company (01823 667242) on page 2.

Wicanders Cork Flooring (01403 710001) on page 31.

Ulster Carpet Mills Ltd (01762 334433) on pages 13, 49, 53.

First published in 1997 by Boxtree
an imprint of Macmillan Publishers Ltd
25 Eccleston Place, London SW1W 9NF
and Basingstoke
Associated companies throughout the world

ISBN 0 7522 1111 0

Text © Boxtree, an imprint of Macmillan Publishers Ltd 1997
Photographs © IPC Magazines Ltd

1 3 5 7 9 8 6 4 2

A CIP catalogue entry for this book is available from the British Library.

Front cover photographs by main picture: Brian North; Insets: Russell Sadur and Dominic Blackmore reproduced courtesy of *Homes & Ideas* magazine and Robert Harding Syndication

Designed by Robert Updegraff
Illustrations by Julia Glynn-Smith
Printed and bound in Italy by Manfrini

Floors and Flooring is one of a series of books published in association with *Homes & Ideas* magazine. Also available are: *Shelving and Storage*, *Children's Rooms* and *Window Dressing*. All the books in the series are available from bookshops, recommended retail price £4.99, or you can order direct from the publisher: Boxtree, an imprint of Macmillan General Books C. S., Book Service by Post, PO Box 29, Douglas I-O-M, IM99 1BQ; tel: 01624 675137; fax: 01624 670923; Internet: http://www.bookpost.co.uk. There is a charge of 75 pence per book for postage and packing. Overseas customers please allow £1.00 per copy for post and packing.

Homes & Ideas is published monthly by Southbank Publishing Group, IPC Magazines Ltd, King's Reach Tower, Stamford Street, London SE1 9LS. For subscription enquiries and overseas orders call 01444–445555 (fax no: 01444–445599). Please send orders, address changes and all correspondence to: IPC Magazines Ltd, Oakfield House, 35 Perrymount Road, Haywards Heath, West Sussex RH16 3DH. All cheques should be made payable to IPC Magazines Ltd. Alternatively, you can call the subscription credit card hotline (UK orders only) on 01622–778778.